WHAT'S THE DEAL?

LSD and Other Hallucinogens

TEENAGE READING

SEFTON LIBRARY SERVICES	
002404275X	
Bertrams	02.11.05
J362.293DRE	£12.50
C	12 NOV 2005

Suzanna Drew-Edwards

Heinemann
LIBRARY

KU-452-155

www.heinemann.co.uk/library

Visit our website to find out more information about Heinemann Library books.

To order:

Phone 44 (0) 1865 888066

Send a fax to 44 (0) 1865 314091

Visit the Heinemann Bookshop at www.heinemann.co.uk/library to browse our catalogue and order online.

Produced for Heinemann Library by
White-Thomson Publishing Ltd,
Bridgewater Business Centre,
210 High Street, Lewes,
East Sussex BN7 2NH.

First published in Great Britain by Heinemann Library,
Jordan Hill, Oxford OX2 8EJ, part of Harcourt Education.

Heinemann Library is a registered trademark of
Harcourt Education Ltd.

© Harcourt Education Ltd 2006
The moral right of the proprietor has been asserted.

All rights reserved. No part of this publication may be
reproduced, stored in a retrieval system, or transmitted
in any form or by any means, electronic, mechanical,
photocopying, recording, or otherwise, without either
the prior written permission of the publishers or a
licence permitting restricted copying in the United
Kingdom issued by the Copyright Licensing Agency Ltd,
90 Tottenham Court Road, London W1T 4LP
(www.cla.co.uk).

Consultant: Jenny McWhirter, Head of Education and
    Prevention, DrugScope
Editorial: Clare Collinson
Design: Tim Mayer
Picture Research: Elaine Fuoco-Lang and Amy Sparks
Production: Duncan Gilbert

Originated by P.T. Repro Multi Warna
Printed and bound in China, by South China
    Printing Company.

The case studies and quotations in this book are
based on factual examples. However, in some cases,
the names or other personal information have been
changed to protect the privacy of the individual
concerned.

ISBN 0 431 10782 3
10 09 08 07 06
10 9 8 7 6 5 4 3 2 1

British Library Cataloguing in Publication Data
Drew-Edwards, Suzanna
    LSD and other hallucinogens. – (What's the deal?)
    1. Hallucinogenic drugs – Juvenile literature
    2. Drug abuse – Juvenile literature
    I. Title
    362.2'94
A full catalogue record for this book is available from
the British Library.

Acknowledgements
The publisher would like to thank the following for
their kind permission to use their photographs:

Alamy Images **13** (David Hoffman), **16** (David Hoffman),
24 (Fredrik Skold), **26** (Eddie Gerald), **29** (Pictor
International), **30–31** (Ulrike Preuss/Photofusion Picture
Library), **34–35** (Acestock), **36–37** (Janine Wiedel), **38**
(Janine Wiedel), **40** (Mikael Karlsson); Corbis **8–9** (Ted
Streshinsky), **14–15** (Scott Houston), **17** (Andrew
Brookes), **19** (Lawrence Manning), **28** (H. David
Seawell), **43** (Reuters), **46–47** (Pete Saloutos), **49** (Nancy
Ney); Getty Images **23** (Stone); Topfoto **6** (Topham
Picturepoint), **7**, **10–11** (National), **12** (Laurie Campbell),
25 (UPP), **33**; Topfoto/The ImageWorks **4–5**, **20–21**, **44**,
45, **48**, **50**.

Cover artwork by Phil Weyman, Kralinator Design.

Every effort has been made to contact copyright
holders of any material reproduced in this book. Any
omissions will be rectified in subsequent printings if
notice is given to the publishers.

The paper used to print this book comes from
sustainable resources.

Contents

▌Words appearing in the text in bold, **like this**, are explained in the Glossary.

LSD and other hallucinogens – what's the deal?

Al is sixteen. Some of his friends use drugs, including the **hallucinogens** LSD and **magic mushrooms**. He doesn't want to try them. Sometimes his friends ask him why, and he finds it difficult to explain.

"Lots of my friends do drugs. They smoke dope and one of them has a brother who can get hold of magic mushrooms and **acid**, so they sometimes take those too. They all make out that it's no big deal, that all the weird feelings you get are cool and there isn't anything wrong with it. They say it's safe as long as you're careful. Sometimes they try to talk me into giving it a go. I don't want to do it. But it's difficult. You feel stupid saying no when you don't really know why you're saying it, especially if they try and convince you it's OK. They probably think I'm scared, but I just don't want to do it."

What would you do if you were Al? One day you may find yourself in a similar situation. What decision will you make?

What are hallucinogens?

Hallucinogens are a group of drugs that change the way people see, feel, and hear the things around them. They cause **hallucinations**, in which someone sees or hears things that seem real but don't exist. LSD (or acid) is probably the best-known hallucinogenic drug. Other hallucinogenic drugs include magic mushrooms, **mescaline**, **PCP** (**phencyclidine**), and **ketamine**.

Hallucinogens can have very powerful effects, which vary from person to person. The most usual effect is known as a "**trip**". Some trips can lead to strong feelings of anxiety and panic – this is known as a "**bad trip**". These drugs are unpredictable – no one knows quite how an experience will affect them.

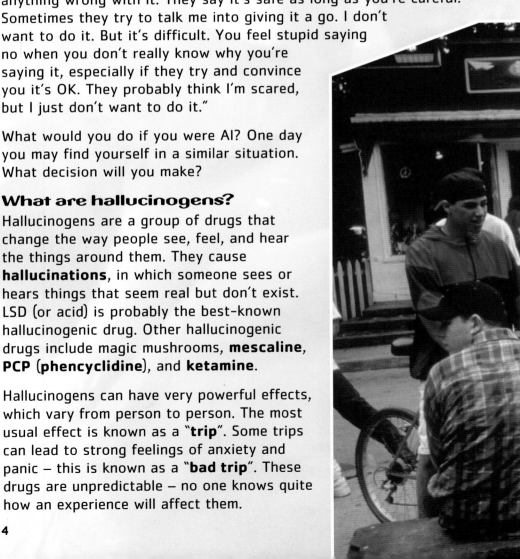

Making decisions

You might think that LSD and other hallucinogens will never be an issue for you. But if you were offered one of these drugs by someone you know, do you know what you would say? This book will give you the information you need to make your own decisions about hallucinogenic drugs.

There are many issues to think about. Why are some people tempted to use these drugs and what harm can they do? Are hallucinogens **addictive** and what are the long-term risks? Let's take a hard look at LSD and other hallucinogens.

❚ Some young people may try hallucinogens because they feel under pressure to fit in with their friends.

LSD is an illegal **psychedelic** (mind-altering) drug derived from a **fungus** called ergot. It is made in laboratories from lysergic acid, a chemical found in ergot. Its full chemical name is Lysergic Acid Diethylamide. It is a very powerful drug that has unpredictable effects on the mind. LSD is usually taken orally (by sucking or eating), and is often found on small squares of perforated paper known as "**blotters**" or "**tabs**".

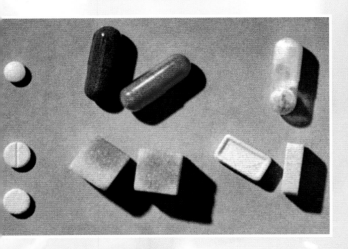

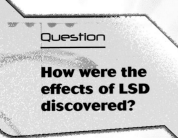

▌LSD can be formed into pills, or dissolved in liquid and absorbed into material such as gelatine.

What does LSD look like?

In its pure state, LSD is a white powder. This is often dissolved in liquid and soaked into a sheet of absorbent paper called blotter paper. When the liquid evaporates, the LSD is left embedded in the fibres of the paper. Blotter sheets are often decorated with artwork such as smiley faces, strawberries, rockets, and so on. A typical single-dose blotter or tab is just under a centimetre (0.3 inches) square. More rarely, LSD comes in the form of small pills (called microdots), on sheets of **gelatine**, or as a liquid that is sometimes dropped on to sugar cubes.

LSD in medicine

In the 1950s, LSD was used in the study and treatment of mental illness. Doctors believed that the **hallucinogenic** effects of the drug could help some mentally ill patients recall hidden feelings. Some doctors also believed that LSD might be a cure for **schizophrenia**

Question

How were the effects of LSD discovered?

(a **psychological** illness), alcoholism, and criminal behaviour. LSD is no longer used medically. In the United Kingdom, medical use of the drug came to an end in 1971 with the Misuse of Drugs Act, and in the United States it ended in 1970, with the Controlled Substances Act.

Non-medical use

LSD began to be used for non-medical reasons (also known as **recreational use**) in the 1960s when some people, especially **hippies**, thought it gave them a spiritual experience and enabled them to "explore their minds". The drug was made illegal in the United Kingdom in 1966 and in the United States in 1967. You can read more about the recreational use of LSD today on pages 10–11.

█ Street names for LSD

Street names for LSD include: **acid**, blotters, cheer, dots, drop, flash, hawk, L, lightning flash, liquid acid, lucy, paper mushrooms, rainbows, smilies, stars, sugar, sunshine, tab, trips, and window.

▌ Blotter sheets may look like innocent and groovy artwork, but they carry a dangerous and illegal drug.

Answer

The effects of LSD were first discovered in 1943 by a Swiss chemist called Albert Hofmann. He had been researching the fungus ergot and by accident took some LSD and experienced a psychedelic **trip**.

What does LSD do?

LSD has unpredictable effects that vary from person to person, and it can affect the same person in different ways on different occasions. How a person reacts depends on factors such as how much of the drug has been taken and the mood of the user. No one can know in advance if a **trip** will be a bad one, and once a trip has started it cannot be stopped.

Question

What are flashbacks?

LSD distorts the way the mind perceives things. Colours may seem brighter, noises louder, and visual images can change without warning. Time may seem to speed up or slow down. A person may experience **hallucinations**, which is when they see images, hear sounds, and feel things that seem real but don't exist.

People may also experience strong feelings of fear and anxiety. You can read more about the effects of tripping on pages 24–31.

In the long term, LSD can also cause unwanted **side effects**, including frightening **flashbacks**. It can also cause mental or **psychological** illnesses such as anxiety, depression, and **paranoia** (when someone becomes suspicious for no good reason, or feels that people are "out to get them"). You can find out more about the health risks of LSD and other **hallucinogens** on pages 32–35.

Answer

Flashbacks are when someone suddenly re-experiences some of the hallucinogenic effects of a trip. They may involve terrifying visual disturbances and can occur days, weeks, or even years after the person experienced the initial trip.

"It was the first time that I'd tried LSD. We were in my friend's bedroom when I had half a **tab** of **acid** and for a while nothing seemed to happen. Then colours began to get more vivid and noises seemed clearer ... then it all took a sharp turn. My friend changed the CD and the music sounded doomed and forbidding. I felt overwhelmed with panic, I couldn't speak ... everything was out of control. I lay on the floor in my friend's room in a nightmare and I felt like I was losing myself ... going mad. I was up all night hoping beyond everything that I'd get through this hell."

Ben, aged seventeen

▌LSD distorts the senses and changes the way a person sees, hears, and feels.

LSD was a popular **recreational** drug during the 1960s, but use of the drug decreased from the mid-1970s onwards. In the late 1980s, there was a renewed interest in **hallucinogenic** drugs, coinciding with the rise in the popularity of all-night dance parties called **raves**. Recent reports suggest that the number of young people using LSD today is decreasing, and it is usually taken in smaller doses than in the 1960s. However, even in small doses, LSD can have very frightening effects.

Changing patterns

Nowadays, a typical **tab** might contain about 50 micrograms of LSD, whereas in the 1960s, the amount taken could be as much as 250–300 micrograms. According to present-day drug **counsellors**, teenagers today are more likely to use LSD for an "experimental" experience, rather than aiming for the full-blown spiritual experience users were hoping for in the 1960s. Some young users today experiment with the drug once and never use it again. However, just one low dose of LSD can still provoke strong, uncontrollable reactions and lasting after-effects such as **flashbacks**.

How many people use LSD?

Today, very few people use LSD, particularly when compared to other drugs such as ecstasy or cocaine. Recent reports have shown that the use of LSD is decreasing. "Monitoring the Future" is a research programme carried out at the University of Michigan in the United States. It was set up in 1975 to track the use of illegal drugs among high-school

I Although use of LSD is decreasing, it is sometimes used at raves and rock concerts.

students in the United States. The most recent survey, from 2003, reported a dramatic drop in the use of LSD. The number of high-school students who had used the drug once or more in their lifetime nearly halved between 2001 and 2003. It is thought that this trend may be the result of successful police operations that have disrupted the production and supply of the drug. You can read more about these operations on pages 42–43.

! LSD use today

Most young people have never tried LSD. Recent reports have shown that:

- in the United Kingdom, only 0.8 per cent of 16 to 24-year-olds had used LSD in the last year

- in the United States, only 1.6 per cent of high-school students had used LSD in the last year.

LSD is one member of a large group of **hallucinogenic** drugs. Others include **magic mushrooms**, **ketamine**, **mescaline**, and **PCP** (phencyclidine). They all cause the user to **trip** in slightly different ways and all can be dangerous to use.

Magic mushrooms

Magic mushrooms are from the same family as LSD and are non-poisonous **fungi** that contain the chemicals psilocybin and psilocin. They grow wild in many parts of the world and are eaten fresh or dried, or drunk in tea or soup. They bring about a similar, but shorter, tripping experience to LSD. Over 90 kinds of magic mushrooms exist worldwide, but the most common type is the Liberty Cap.

! Street names for magic mushrooms

Street names for magic mushrooms include: shrooms, liberties, magics, caps, and mushies.

▌ Some wild mushrooms are poisonous enough to cause death. Eaten in large quantities, fly agaric mushrooms like these can lead to heart failure.

One of the dangers of taking mushrooms is that they are very difficult to identify. Many mushrooms are poisonous. How can someone know if they have the right kind?

There are a number of other **psychedelic** mushrooms, including fly agaric mushrooms. These are very poisonous and have dangerous **side effects**. It is extremely difficult to identify magic mushrooms. Thousands of different types grow in the wild and some are poisonous enough to cause death within hours of eating them. All too often, users confuse magic mushrooms with poisonous, sometimes deadly, fungi.

As with all hallucinogenic drugs, the effects of magic mushrooms are unpredictable. They vary from person to person and depend on the amount taken. A trip can be very unsettling and some people suffer from frightening **flashbacks**.

Nicola's story

Taking magic mushrooms can sometimes make people feel confused, anxious, and frightened. This is what happened to Nicola, who was given some magic mushrooms by her boyfriend.

"I had a terrible experience on shrooms. I felt fine at first and then all of a sudden I felt extreme anxiety. I have never been so scared in my life. I felt like I was fighting with myself. I started screaming at my boyfriend. Everything I saw was changing and I didn't know where I was. I was being really mean to him one second and the next second I was apologizing, trying to tell him I didn't mean it. I could not understand anything that was going on. I had no concept of anything. Even time. Literally a minute felt like it should have been two or three hours."

Ketamine

Ketamine is an **anaesthetic** drug that has been used to make humans and animals unconscious before surgery, and to reduce pain. It is also used as a "club drug" on the all-night dance scene. Users sometimes call the drug "K" or "special K". Ketamine can cause people to enter a trance-like state and experience **hallucinations**. A large dose of ketamine can bring on a terrifying effect known as a "K hole", where someone can feel as if they are totally separated from what is going on around them. Sometimes a person may not even be able to move their arms or legs. Large doses may cause a person to become unconscious.

> *"It took me back to when I was under anaesthetic for a dental operation. I didn't like it."*
>
> Dan, who tried ketamine at the age of seventeen

Recently there have been cases of sexual assault and rape involving the use of ketamine, as well as other drugs such as Rohypnol ("roofies") and GHB (Gamma Hydroxybutyrate). The drug may be slipped into a person's drink or food without them knowing (this is known as "spiking"), and the drug's effects make the person physically and mentally unable to defend themselves. The victim may become unconscious and when they wake up they may not even know that they have been raped.

▌ Ketamine is increasingly being used as a club drug, but in high doses it can make people completely disorientated.

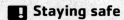
▉ Staying safe

There are several things people can do to reduce the risk of drug-assisted rape. They should:

- never accept drinks from strangers

- never leave a drink unattended

- never share drinks with other people

- buy bottled drinks and keep the lid on them when not drinking out of them

- stop drinking a drink if it looks or tastes strange.

Mescaline
Mescaline is a strong **hallucinogen** extracted from the top of the peyote cactus, which grows in Mexico. Mescaline can also be produced **synthetically**. The drug can make someone feel confused and disorientated, and they may have intense and sometimes terrifying hallucinations. They may also experience anxiety, dizziness, increased blood pressure and heart rate, nausea, and shivering.

Salvia divinorum
Salvia divinorum is a green plant belonging to the mint family. Its leaves are sometimes smoked or chewed, causing users to experience short-lived effects (lasting one hour or less), including intense hallucinations. In high doses, users can enter a completely uncontrollable state and in some cases they become unconscious. Little is known about how this drug works on the brain, but some experts believe that in the long term it can cause mental illness.

PCP

PCP (**phencyclidine**), sometimes known as "angel dust", is a **synthetically** produced **hallucinogen** that comes in liquid, crystal, pill, or powder form. It can be smoked in a cigarette (often with cannabis), **snorted** (sniffed up through the nose), swallowed, or injected. PCP is a highly dangerous drug that has many unpleasant physical effects, including nausea, blurred vision, numbness, dizziness, and increased blood pressure and heart rate. It also triggers **hallucinations**, violent behaviour, anxiety, and **paranoia**. Users of PCP may experience mental disturbances that can last for days or weeks. High doses can cause seizures (fits), **coma**, and death. In the long term, PCP users sometimes have memory and speech difficulties.

❙ PCP is manufactured in illegal laboratories, and the tablets often contain chemical impurities.

DMT

DMT (**dimethyltriptamine**) is a hallucinogenic drug that acts quickly and produces a strong **trip** lasting between ten minutes and an hour. It is normally smoked, snorted, or injected. DMT can cause serious **side effects**, including increased heart rate and blood pressure, nausea, insomnia, and confusion.

DXM

DXM (**dextromethorphan**) is found in some cough syrups and pills. Large doses can cause bad visual hallucinations, slurred speech, uncoordinated movements, and unconsciousness. An **overdose** can result in coma and death. Taking any medicine in larger-than-recommended doses is extremely dangerous. **Pharmacists** are required to take note of someone buying large quantities of cough syrups.

Other relatively new synthetic hallucinogens include:

- **2C–T–7** – this drug can cause long-lasting and overwhelming visual hallucinations. Users sometimes also experience anxiety, mental confusion, and violent reactions. In high doses it can cause death.

- **5–MeO–DiPT** (Foxy, Foxy Methoxy) – reactions to this drug vary dramatically. Some users experience nausea, diarrhoea, anxiety, muscle tension, and restlessness.

- **AMT (alpha–methyltryptamine)** – this is a very dangerous synthetic substance that has effects that last from 8 to 24 hours. AMT can cause hallucinations, distortion of the senses, nausea, and vomiting.

- **Nexus** or **2CB** – this drug is related to the drug ecstasy, although 2CB is more powerful. The effects depend on the amount taken. Users may experience frightening hallucinations, confusion, anxiety, **panic attacks**, depression, and heart problems.

❗ **The dangers of PCP**

In the United States, more people need emergency medical treatment after taking PCP than any other hallucinogen. Recent studies have shown that the number is increasing. In 2002, over 7500 people visited emergency departments after taking PCP – this was 42 per cent more than in 2000.

❚ Most cough syrups and pills that contain DXM also contain other ingredients that can be very dangerous, even deadly, if taken in large doses.

So who takes LSD and other **hallucinogens**? Most people do not take illegal drugs of any kind, but it seems that the use of hallucinogens is most common among people aged between 18 and 25. In the 1960s, hallucinogens were used as part of the **hippy** culture, but nowadays they are often referred to as "club drugs". This is because they are sometimes used by people at dance parties and **raves**.

"You hear so much about drugs – at school, friends, films, music lyrics … everything – that it makes you want to try them out. They're a part of life for lots of people who are just like me."

Chris, aged fifteen. In fact, most young people never take illegal drugs. Chris may think that if he tries an illegal drug he can control it, rather than have it controlling him. But if he knew the reality of what hallucinogenic drugs could do to him, it might make him think again.

How many people take hallucinogens?

In the United States, recent research has reported that 23 per cent of people aged between 18 and 25 have experimented with hallucinogens at least once in their lifetime. But it seems that far fewer people are regular users of hallucinogens – only 1.7 per cent of people of this age had used the drug in the last month.

Among younger people aged between twelve and seventeen, the use of hallucinogens is less common. In this age group, 5 per cent of people reported that they had experimented with hallucinogenic drugs during their lifetime, and 1 per cent had used them in the last month. The research also suggested that males are twice as likely to be regular users of hallucinogens than females.

Question

Is the use of hallucinogens increasing?

▌Hallucinogen use today is often linked to clubs and raves.

In the United Kingdom, the British Crime Survey figures for 2003 suggest that these drugs are most commonly used among people aged between 20 and 24. In that age group, 1.4 per cent of people had used LSD in the past year and 2.2 per cent had used **magic mushrooms**.

In Australia, figures for 2001 show that 7.6 per cent of people aged 14 and over had used hallucinogens at some stage in their life and 1.1 per cent had used them in the past year.

Answer

No. While use of hallucinogens increased during the 1990s, recent research in the United States and the United Kingdom suggests that the number of people using hallucinogens is now decreasing.

What is it that drives some people to take **hallucinogenic** drugs? Some people may try them out of curiosity or because they want to be rebellious. Others may try the drugs because they have been offered them by their friends and they can't think of a reason to say no. When people are offered hallucinogens, they are often told that the drugs are completely safe. In reality, taking hallucinogens carries all kinds of risks.

A risky adventure?

Some people may be tempted to try hallucinogens because they want to be daring and rebellious. To a curious "risk-taking" person, the fact that hallucinogens are strong drugs with mind-warping properties may be enough to make them sound interesting enough to try. Often, these people do not realize quite how variable hallucinogenic drugs are and what terrifying effects they can have. Once they see the reality of what these drugs can do, many people are put off and never use hallucinogens again.

▌Some people may feel under pressure to try hallucinogens when drugs are passed round among friends at clubs.

Joining in?

Some young people may try hallucinogens because they feel under pressure from their friends or other people they know. They may be at a party or at a dance club where drugs are being passed around. They may think that if they don't join in with the group activity, their friends may start to drift away to be with those who do want to join in.

What is important to remember in this situation is that people should be free to make their own decisions about drugs. A true friend accepts you as you are.

Viewpoints

Some people think that drugs education for people who are at school is a good idea and will help to reduce the number of young people who use drugs. Others strongly disagree.

- ## Educating young people about drugs helps them make wiser decisions

Sometimes children are offered drugs at a very young age, so many people believe that drugs education should start at a young age too. If young people understand the dangers of these drugs they will have a good reason and more confidence to say no.

- ## Drugs education introduces young people to drugs too soon

Some people argue that educating young people about drugs might make them want to learn more about drugs and their effects. They may get ideas that they would not otherwise have had, and be more interested in trying them. Many people also believe younger children should not be told about drugs because they are not old enough to understand about them. They argue it would be better just to say that drugs are dangerous and illegal.

What do you think?

Hallucinogens – the supply network

Most people who use **hallucinogens** do not buy their drugs from **dealers** on the street. They are more likely to obtain the drugs from people they know. But there is still a dealer in the background **supplying** the drugs for profit. Just because someone is given drugs by a friend, it does not mean that they are safe to use.

At street level, hallucinogens may be bought from dealers at clubs or at rock venues. But people who use hallucinogens usually obtain them in small quantities from friends, brothers, or sisters. They will often use them at home or at a friend's house.

To some people, the fact that LSD and other hallucinogens are passed round amongst a group of friends may make it seem like one big friendly "club". However, friends are often unaware of the health risks of these drugs and may give bad advice. Even though there may be a number of friends or acquaintances involved in the supply chain, the distribution network always includes a drug dealer who is selling illegal substances for financial gain.

"My brother's friend Dave had some mushrooms which he sold to my brother and me. But Dave was out that night and was picked up by the police. When they searched him they found some of the mushrooms and a sheet of **blotters**. He may have to face court proceedings. His parents know and he's worried that legal action may affect his future at college."

Mark, aged fourteen

Buying illegal drugs – the risks

When someone buys illegal drugs, they can never be sure what they're getting. This applies to drugs obtained from friends as well as drugs bought from a dealer on the street or at a club. Illegal drugs are not subject to any kind of quality control, so it is impossible to be certain about the strength of the drugs. Any illegal drug may contain chemical impurities, as dealers often mix the drugs with other cheaper ingredients so they can make more profit.

The legal risk

People who pass on illegal drugs to their friends, even for no money, are breaking the law. The legal risks of using and supplying drugs are very serious. Even if a person "looks after" LSD and other hallucinogenic drugs for a friend and then hands them back, they could face a prison sentence. You can read more about the laws on hallucinogens on pages 40–41.

❚ Most young people don't use illegal drugs. But young people who use hallucinogens usually get them from their friends.

The term "**tripping**" came about after the first LSD users described the experience as a "trip inside the mind". So what is this like for people? Is it a pleasant experience? The truth is that no one can know how tripping will affect them, and once a trip starts there's nothing anyone can do to stop it. It can be a terrifying experience, when people see things that seem real but don't really exist. These may be things such as spiders, blood, insects, monsters, and skulls. A **bad trip** can be like your worst nightmare come to life.

What will it be like?

You can never tell what's going to happen when you take **hallucinogens**. More than with any other drug, the effects of hallucinogens vary from person to person and from one occasion to another.

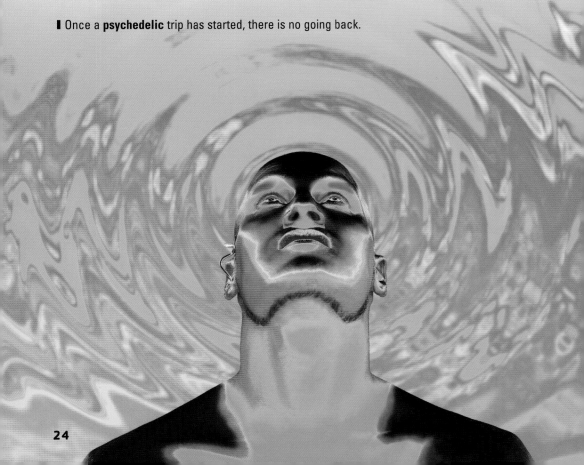

❚ Once a **psychedelic** trip has started, there is no going back.

■ Hallucinogenic trips can make people see frightening images of things that aren't really there.

❗ What are the physical signs of tripping?

Tripping distorts the senses and can have strong effects on the emotions, but there are also physical effects. These include:

- dilated pupils

- increased body temperature, heart rate, and blood pressure

- feelings of nausea

- shivering, sweating, and shaking

- dry mouth

- numbness

- lack of coordination

- abnormal breathing.

The effects depend on many things, including:

- how much of the drug is taken

- the user's height and weight

- the user's mood and expectations

- whether the person is used to taking the drug

- whether other drugs, including alcohol, have also been taken

- the environment the person is in.

Just because someone didn't have a bad experience the last time, it doesn't mean they won't the next time.

The effects of tripping

The first effects of hallucinogens may include a feeling of "strangeness" filling the body. Senses may be distorted. Colours may seem more vivid and sounds become louder. By this time, the user has probably realized they are feeling the effects of the drug, but if they don't like them, it's too late. Once a trip has taken hold, a person is under its spell until the trip is over. Depending on the drug taken, this could be for twelve hours or more.

Bad trips

When a trip is dominated by negative thoughts, it can have traumatic effects on the user's emotions. Some users may find the trip feels OK to begin with and then takes a terrifying turn — they may start to see teeth sprouting all over someone's face, or a head with two faces. Noises can become painfully loud.

▌Some people don't realize that during a hallucinogenic trip even a "good" experience can suddenly become terrifying.

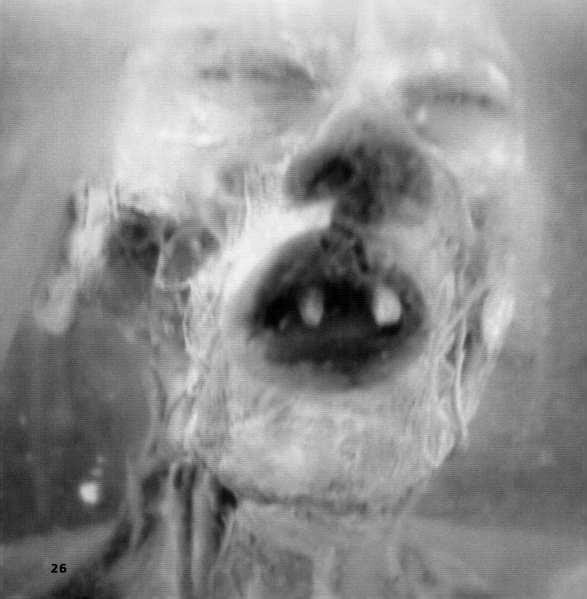

A **bad trip** can make someone swing rapidly from one emotion to another – for example, from panic and hysteria to uncontrollable fear and back to panic again. Experiencing a bad trip can leave a person feeling very shaken and it may cause anxiety and **paranoia**. Anxiety may trigger breathlessness or even a full-blown **panic attack**.

What causes a bad trip?

No one fully understands why people experience bad trips. However, it seems they are more likely to happen if the user is depressed or anxious before taking the drug, or if the user isn't in relaxed surroundings. If they feel uncomfortable, they may recall unpleasant memories or have "bad" thoughts. Bad trips seem to be particularly common among first-time users of **hallucinogens**.

*"I was out with a friend who had got hold of some **blotters**. I wasn't sure, but was persuaded to tear one in half and try. At first everything just got louder, more obvious. I was stupid and took the other half. Then my mind started crawling inside itself – that's the only way I can explain it. I was screaming inside, and although my friend tried to help, she couldn't. She had snakes coming from her fingernails – I was petrified of her. I huddled in a ball for what seemed like hours."*

Louise, who tried LSD once

⚠ What do I do in an emergency situation?

If you're with someone who appears to be in trouble after taking a hallucinogenic drug, don't try to handle the situation on your own. Call an ambulance and explain what has happened. You won't get into trouble. While you're waiting for the ambulance to arrive:

- stay calm and don't panic

- stay with the person – do not leave them alone

- talk to the person, remind them who they are and who you are

- remind the person to breathe and to relax – they will probably be feeling confused, anxious, and frightened.

When the paramedics arrive, give them as much information as you can – for example, which hallucinogen the person has taken, how much, and how long ago.

■ Experiencing a hallucinogenic trip is like being on an express train. You can't get off until the journey's over – no matter how bad it makes you feel.

Does LSD make you think you can fly?

No, not really. It is, however, a very powerful mind-altering drug that can make someone believe they can do things they can't, so they may misjudge the height from which they are able to jump.

A mystery tour

Because LSD and other **hallucinogens** are so unpredictable, a user can never foresee which way a **trip** will turn. They may think they know their body and how strong a dose they can tolerate, but other factors can all affect the route their tripping experience will take.

A person taking LSD or other hallucinogens may be aiming for a "slow bus ride", but could find out they've got on to a "high speed train" by mistake. The hallucinogenic effects of these drugs may last for many hours, so the trip can become worse as a person's environment changes. Someone may start off their trip in the safety of their own home, surrounded by friends, for example. But going outside that safe haven can cause the trip to become a terrifying experience. When you consider how long a trip can go on for, it is very likely that someone will not be in the same place for the duration of their trip. Even something as simple as walking into a room that is full of unfamiliar faces can be extremely frightening – the user may feel overwhelming **paranoia** and the unfamiliar faces may change into ghoulish spectres.

What are the risks of tripping?

Tripping can make someone less aware of risks, and activities that need coordination, such as swimming, can be very dangerous. Someone who is having a **bad trip** is particularly at risk. Panic can trigger dangerous behaviour, such as racing across a busy road. It has been known for injuries and fatal accidents to occur while people are under the influence of hallucinogens.

▌Tripping on hallucinogens may make someone think they can do the impossible .

▉ The dangers of mixing drugs

People who use hallucinogens often combine them with other drugs, which can be very risky. For example, LSD may well be taken at the same time as **magic mushrooms**, cannabis, or ecstasy. The dangers of any drug are increased if it is taken at the same time as another drug or while another drug is still in the body. It is particularly risky to mix hallucinogens with alcohol or **amphetamines**. Combining **PCP** with alcohol can kill.

Once someone has taken a **hallucinogenic** drug, there is nothing they can do to stop its effects. These effects can last for more than twelve hours and it then takes time for the person to recover. Carrying out activities, such as driving, cycling, catching a bus, or operating machinery, is dangerous when **intoxicated**, so normal daily life while under the influence of these drugs is impossible.

Hallucinogens – the time-wasters

Many people who take hallucinogenic drugs don't take them on a regular basis and daily use of hallucinogens is rare. Most users take them at weekends or on occasions that may be months apart. **Tripping** on LSD takes over mind and body for at least twelve hours and a user is often left exhausted by the experience, yet unable to sleep. People need a long time to recover.

For an LSD user about to take a **tab**, the trip that follows is going to be the only thing that happens during that day or night. Studying at school or college, or carrying out a job, cannot happen – because tripping makes it impossible. The experience begins with the user waiting for the trip to happen. Once it starts, the person will be unable to do anything other than experience the effects. Doing anything that doesn't feel comfortable can turn a trip into a nightmare.

Other hallucinogenic substances may not take over daily life for the same length of time as LSD, but they can still have an extreme effect on how people feel and how able they are to get on with their everyday lives. **Magic mushrooms** produce a shorter (four to six hours), but potentially intense, tripping experience which can leave a person exhausted and feeling **paranoid**. As with LSD, **bad trips** on magic mushrooms can lead to **flashbacks** and panic.

■ Flashbacks happen without warning and can be very frightening.

Flashbacks may be triggered by a particular sight or sound. They may also happen if someone is stressed or tired. Flashbacks can occur after someone has used the drug once, but they become more common if someone uses hallucinogens a lot. Flashbacks also become more likely if someone mixes hallucinogens with other drugs, such as ecstasy, cannabis, or alcohol.

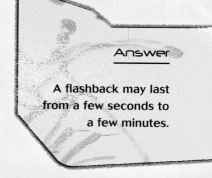

Answer

A flashback may last from a few seconds to a few minutes.

Longer-term psychological problems

Bad trips and **flashbacks** aren't the only risks of **hallucinogens**. Because these are such powerful mind-altering drugs, they can have lasting harmful **psychological** effects. While many users have continuing feelings of despair and **paranoia** after a bad trip has ended, some users experience longer-term psychological problems. These problems include depression and **schizophrenia**.

Nobody really knows whether hallucinogens actually cause these psychological problems, or whether they just trigger a pre-existing underlying mental illness in some people. What is known is that people with a family history of mental illnesses such as schizophrenia should not use hallucinogens. If someone who already suffers from these conditions takes hallucinogens, it may make their symptoms worse.

Question

Does LSD make you go mad?

▌The long-term effects of hallucinogens can include serious visual disturbances.

Celeste's story

Celeste started taking LSD at the age of fifteen and continued on a regular basis for some time. When she started getting bad trips she decided to stop, but she is still experiencing some long-term effects.

*"I was fine for three years, then one day, I was out to lunch with my dad. I stood up, the ground shifted, I felt that heat wave of an **acid trip** come over me and I hit the floor. I was **hallucinating** so badly I had no idea where I was. I have spent the last two-and-a-half years trying to figure out what is wrong with me. My symptoms include visual distortions and pressure in my head ... and my symptoms worsen when I exercise or drink. I am only 23, and I pray for a cure."*

HPPD

Some users suffer from a condition called HPPD (Hallucinogen Persisting Perception Disorder). This is a condition which involves long-term visual disturbances. People suffering from HPPD may see stationary objects "sliding" back and forth, geometric patterns on objects, or "floaters", which are like dark dots or shadowy lines in the sky. Some users experience these disturbances frequently and it can seriously interfere with their daily lives. This disorder may slowly fade away, but it can sometimes last for more than ten years.

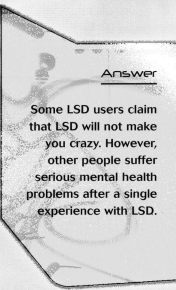

Answer

Some LSD users claim that LSD will not make you crazy. However, other people suffer serious mental health problems after a single experience with LSD.

All **hallucinogens** can quickly lead to **tolerance**. This is when somebody who uses a drug frequently has to take larger and larger doses in order to feel the same effects. Hallucinogens are very powerful drugs that have unpredictable effects, so taking large doses can be very risky.

Question

What is tolerance?

Hallucinogens and tolerance

People can develop tolerance to many kinds of drugs, but with hallucinogens, tolerance can develop very quickly. For example, if someone were to take LSD every day for three or four days, even very high doses of the drug would have no effect whatsoever. Trying to overcome the effects of tolerance by taking larger and

Dex's story

Dex, aged nineteen, first took LSD at sixteen. He found that after a year of taking LSD every weekend, it no longer had the same effect.

"I used to take LSD in **blotter** *form every weekend – sometimes twice a week. I started with one-blotter doses and, one year later, I was on about six blotters a* **trip**. *After a while I realized my mind-expanding trips were getting less effective and less out of this world. I was taking more blotters to try to get the same effects. As I carried on, the after-effects seemed to take over – and the quality of trips wasn't making up for the negatives. I don't want to go through nine hours of aching cramps in my back and legs and negative thoughts where everyone hates me again."*

larger doses of a drug is extremely dangerous. This is true of any drug, but particularly true of drugs as unpredictable as hallucinogens. After a period of not taking the drug, tolerance goes away and the effects of the drug can be felt again. Other hallucinogens such as **ketamine**, **DMT**, and **magic mushrooms** also produce tolerance. If someone uses these drugs within three to four days of a previous use, the drugs will have no effect on their mind.

Cross-tolerance

Becoming tolerant to one kind of hallucinogen can make people tolerant to other kinds. This is called cross-tolerance. For example, LSD use can cause cross-tolerance to **mescaline**, magic mushrooms, and DMT.

Answer

Tolerance is when the body becomes used to the presence of a drug in its system. This means that higher and higher doses are needed to create the same effect as before.

▌ Becoming tolerant may make someone use higher and higher doses of hallucinogens. This may cause long-term psychological problems such as depression.

Addiction or **dependence** is when a person has an unhealthy habit that they feel unable to give up. This habit could be anything from smoking cigarettes to gambling or drinking too much alcohol. But can people become addicted to **hallucinogenic** drugs?

What are addiction and dependence?

Some drugs cause physical addiction. This is when a person's body becomes so used to the drug that when they stop using it they become physically ill with **withdrawal symptoms**. For example, they may have

▌If someone becomes psychologically dependent on a hallucinogen, it can make them feel that life isn't bearable without it.

stomach upsets or flu-like symptoms, or they may start shaking. People may also develop mental or **psychological dependence** on drugs. This is when someone feels an overwhelming desire to continue using the drug to get through everyday life, and feels they cannot cope without it.

Hallucinogens and dependence

Hallucinogens are not thought to cause physical addiction, but they are known to cause psychological dependence in some users. Past experiences with these drugs may make some people feel they need the drugs in order to cope, so they may use them on a regular basis. When someone is psychologically dependent on a drug, it can be hard for them to give it up. You can read more about giving up hallucinogens on pages 48–49.

Viewpoints

Some people may say it's OK to experiment with hallucinogens, such as LSD, because they don't make people physically addicted in the same way as some other drugs. But others argue that psychological dependence on drugs can be just as harmful as physical addiction.

- **Psychological dependence is just as damaging as physical addiction**

When someone is psychologically dependent on a drug, they can become so dependent on the feelings they get from using it that they can't manage emotionally without it. So the drugs begin to control their lives. It can be just as hard for them to stop using the drug as it is for people who are physically addicted to a drug.

- **Physical addiction is more damaging than psychological dependence**

When someone is physically addicted to a drug, it's not just their mind that is dependent on it. Their whole body needs the drug in order to work properly, so they need to keep taking it to feel OK. When they stop taking the drug, they suffer very unpleasant withdrawal symptoms. This makes it much harder for them to give it up.

What do you think?

So what does the law say about **hallucinogens**? Did you know that you can get a criminal record even if you simply look after some illegal drugs for a friend? Or that a criminal record can affect your chances of going to university and getting a good job?

LSD and other hallucinogens are illegal drugs and there are strict penalties for **possessing**, **supplying**, and making these drugs. LSD, psilocybin (contained in **magic mushrooms**), and other hallucinogens, such as **mescaline** and **DMT**, are classified as "Class A" in the United Kingdom and "Schedule 1" in the United States. This means they are recognized as among the most dangerous drugs that can be used. It is illegal to use, possess, sell, or produce them.

▌ If someone is caught in possession of hallucinogens, they may get a criminal record and they may be sent to prison.

Possession

When someone is caught with an illegal drug for their own use, they are guilty of an offence known as possession. The drug doesn't have to be in their pocket or bag, but could be in their house or personal locker. If the person is under seventeen, the police can tell their parents or carer, and they may issue a warning or a formal caution which is entered into police files. A person may also be charged, and if the court finds them guilty they may be fined or sent to prison. They are more likely to be given a prison sentence if they have committed a drug offence before.

Possession with intent to supply

Supplying illegal drugs to others (and this includes giving, not just selling, drugs to friends) is considered a more serious offence than possession. If a person is found guilty in court, the penalty may well be more severe. Even carrying a couple of **tabs** can be classed as possession with intent to supply.

Viewpoints

People can't agree about how to approach the illegal drugs situation. Some people support a "zero-tolerance" approach and think that anyone caught using illegal drugs should be sent to prison. Others think that drug users should be treated for their drug problem rather than punished.

- ## All people caught using drugs should pay a penalty

Illegal drug use is a crime. Punishing drug users, even those who only occasionally use drugs, is one of the best ways of sending out an anti-drug message. Then, anyone who uses illegal drugs will know what will happen if they are caught.

- ## Drug use should be treated as a health problem – not criminal behaviour

Using a law enforcement approach to drugs doesn't help most users – but can make the problem worse. If all users were sent to prison, there would be serious over-crowding issues. While in prison these people might be exposed to more drugs and learn about other criminal activities. The best way to deal with the drugs problem is to help people stop taking them.

What do you think?

The total number of drug users in the world is now estimated at around 185 million people – equivalent to 3 per cent of the global population. The drugs trade is very big business, involving a worldwide network of manufacturers, processors, smugglers, **dealers**, and users. In comparison with cocaine and heroin, LSD and other **hallucinogens** make much smaller profits, and form a less significant part of the worldwide trade in drugs.

❗ The largest LSD lab ever

On 31 March 2003, two men in Kansas, United States, were convicted of running what the US Drug Enforcement Administration called the largest LSD laboratory ever raided in the United States. Leonard Pickard, 57, and Clyde Apperson, 47, had been producing what the authorities said was a third of the country's LSD in a former Kansas nuclear missile silo. Pickard was sentenced to life imprisonment without parole. Apperson was sentenced to 30 years' imprisonment without parole. In the two years after their arrest in 2000, LSD availability in the United States was reduced by 95 per cent.

Where are hallucinogens produced?

LSD has been manufactured illegally since the 1960s by a small number of chemists (known as "cooks"). Manufacturing LSD is time-consuming and dangerous, and sophisticated laboratory equipment is needed. The US Drug Enforcement Administration (DEA) believes that there are now probably fewer than a dozen "cooks" who are manufacturing nearly all the LSD available in the United States. **Synthetic** hallucinogens such as **PCP**, **AMT**, and **Nexus (2CB)** are also produced in illegal laboratories. **Magic mushrooms** are difficult to grow and store, and producers usually grow and distribute the mushrooms locally.

Distribution

The chemists who manufacture hallucinogens don't necessarily take part in distributing the drug. Instead they may sell the drugs to one or two associates who may distribute the drugs by mail order. Once the drugs reach street level, they may be sold at rock concert venues,

raves, or clubs. Addresses and mobile numbers may be traded and these contacts are then used to set up future dealings. This method of distribution means that the sellers are virtually unknown to the buyers. This makes it difficult for drug law enforcement agencies to track down high-level operators.

Law enforcement

Governments and police forces around the world work hard to prevent the production and distribution of LSD and other hallucinogens. Recently, many countries have introduced strict border controls to prevent drugs from being smuggled from one country to another. Recent law enforcement measures in the United States have had a significant impact on the availability of LSD in the United States.

▌Specially trained drug squads, sometimes working with sniffer dogs, operate in many areas, trying to track down drug smugglers and dealers.

The consequences of using LSD and other **hallucinogens** are wide-ranging. These drugs affect the freedom and development of young people and represent a serious threat to health and wellbeing. But using hallucinogens doesn't just affect the users themselves. It also causes problems and stress to many others, especially families and friends. Seeing a child, friend, or relative seriously ill from drug use can have a traumatic effect on someone's life.

Drug use and the family

A regular user of LSD and other hallucinogens may not show the signs of drug use in the same way as, for example, someone who is **addicted** to heroin. A person's family might even be unaware that they are using hallucinogens and that it could have a disastrous effect on their life. They may not find out until it's too late, when their loved one is suffering the long-term consequences of using these drugs.

❙ When someone uses drugs regularly, it can put a serious strain on even the closest of friendships.

Sometimes people may find it better to break away from a group of friends than suffer the pressure to conform.

Friends and friendships

Friends and friendships can also be hurt. Some users are able to hide the truth about their drug use from their family, but the friends of a regular drug user may be more aware of what's going on in that person's life. Friends are often the ones who are confided in. They may be called upon to support someone who is having a **bad trip** and experiencing disturbing **hallucinations**, or they may have to try to control someone who thinks they can jump off a high wall. This kind of situation can be hard for people to cope with.

People who do not use drugs themselves can be affected by someone else's drug use in other ways too. Someone who is friends with a drug user may be anxious that they'll be persuaded into trying the drug. This can put a heavy strain on a friendship, and some people may decide it's better to break a friendship than put up with this pressure.

Greg's story

Greg, 24, is an ex-LSD user. He feels that taking LSD has changed him as a person.

*"I'm a different person since doing **acid**. Sometimes I feel hollow – like I can't smile even if my life depended on it. My college work fell behind for a bit – and I hated doing things I felt were worthless. I've become withdrawn and quieter – and I'm aware that some people find me difficult on a social level. I don't sleep as well as I used to and I pick up bugs and illnesses more frequently."*

LSD and pregnancy

Little is known about whether the use of LSD and other **hallucinogens** during pregnancy can harm an unborn baby. However, taking any drug during pregnancy is risky. The developing tissues of the unborn baby are sensitive to the effects of all drugs. There is evidence that the use of LSD and other hallucinogens during pregnancy can lead to an increased risk of miscarriage. There is also some evidence that the babies of women who use LSD while pregnant are more likely to be born with birth defects.

Medical care

Every year, thousands of people need emergency medical care after taking hallucinogens, and paramedics, doctors, and nurses all have to work hard to care for them. Some users need long-term treatment for the mental health problems they suffer after using hallucinogens. This can mean years of expensive medical care and all these problems take doctors and other health professionals away from their work with other patients.

Dana's story

Dana was on a **prescription medicine** and took LSD and **AMT** together. She had a seizure (fit) and her brother and friends called an ambulance to take her to hospital. She nearly died.

*"I had four seizures on the way to the hospital and was in a **coma** for four days afterwards. My friends thought I had died in the ambulance and my parents had to drive from their home thinking I was either dead or dying. I was in hospital for two weeks afterwards. I've lived to tell the tale, but I've learnt a lot. Like how supportive my family are, although I disappointed them by doing drugs. Like how good my friends are – and what they did for me that night. That's an end of it for me."*

Medical staff face great pressure dealing with emergencies caused by the use of hallucinogens.

The cost of drug crime

Governments all around the world invest large amounts of money in measures to prevent illegal drug use. Society also has to pay for all the work of police officers and customs officers who are trying to prevent the manufacture, distribution, and sale of these drugs. Governments spend huge sums on prosecuting smugglers, **dealers**, and users in court, as well as on keeping them in prison if found guilty.

Giving up hallucinogens

For most people who use **hallucinogens**, there comes a point when they decide they should stop using the drugs. They may decide to stop after a particularly **bad trip** or after experiencing disturbing **flashbacks**. Others may decide to quit when they enter a more responsible period of their lives. Many occasional users of hallucinogenic substances simply decide to decrease or stop their use over time. Whatever the reason for stopping, there is plenty of help available.

How easy is it to stop?

How quickly a user can quit depends on the type of drug, how often they use it, and what sort of person they are. A regular user of hallucinogens who has built up **tolerance** may have a strong **psychological** need for the drug. If LSD or any other hallucinogen has become central to someone's life and what they do, learning how to manage without it and adjusting their mind may take longer.

❚ Stopping using drugs can mean that there's time for new friends and new activities – as well as a healthier lifestyle.

Tony's story

Tony, 24, used hallucinogens over a period of six years. He stopped after experiencing a very disturbing **trip**. After he gave up he found life hard to begin with, but he is now a happier person.

"My final trip two years ago was no fun at all. Although I had tripped many times before with no adverse effects, this one was horrendous. I didn't do it again – it was too much. But the trouble is that when you stop, you've changed. I felt depressed. I lost my job and I didn't work for a year. But things are beginning to improve – I feel I'm a better person. I've found myself a new job in a different field and I'm meeting new people."

Getting help

Fortunately, there is a lot of help available for people who want to stop using drugs. The first step for many people is to talk to a family doctor who can refer them to a drug service. Many people find that talking to a **counsellor** helps. During counselling people can talk about their problems and seek out new ways to express themselves that do not involve drugs. They get help with improving family relationships and mending friendships. There are also many drug agencies that offer advice. Many have useful websites and confidential telephone helplines.

▌ For some, using a drug agency's confidential helpline is the first step to getting help.

Are there things that worry you about LSD and other **hallucinogens**? If there are – either now or in the future – there are lots of people you can contact. There are many organizations that offer help and advice on problems related to drugs. You can call a telephone helpline at any time, and there are trained **counsellors** who can talk through problems and help you find solutions.

▋ Remember – most young people do not use drugs and real friends will respect you if you decide you don't want to use them.

Someone to talk to

Family and friends can be a positive source of help. It's important not to think that just because a person is older, they won't be able to give you advice. Whether it's parents or an aunt or uncle, it's worth talking to people who are close to you.

Sometimes, though, it can be hard to talk to people you know about the things that are worrying you. You may want to discuss your concerns **in confidence**, knowing that whatever you say won't be passed on to anyone you know. You may also feel that you need some expert advice.

Fortunately, there's an easy way to find somebody sympathetic to talk to. Many organizations have telephone helplines, and their phones are staffed by specially trained advisers. And you don't have to be a drug user to call. You can find details of drugs organizations and telephone helplines on pages 54–55 of this book.

It's up to you

Making up your mind about drugs can be difficult. Adults may tell you to "Just say no" – but what happens if it's one of your best friends who is offering you a **tab**? You may not want to try something out, but explaining that to a persuasive friend may be hard. It's important to remember that, whatever some people say, it is OK to say no to drugs. Real friends will always let you make your own decisions and will respect you for them.

❗ Remember ...

If you are worried that some time in the future you might be offered hallucinogens, there are some things you can do to put yourself less at risk.

- Be prepared. Think over what you'll say in advance.

- Never forget the dangers. Taking hallucinogens has serious risks.

- Remember you're not alone. There are a lot of other people your age in the same situation who don't use drugs. And there are always telephone numbers you can call and sympathetic people you can talk to.

- Most of all remember – it's your life. Nobody else can tell you what to do. It's up to you to make your own decisions.

Glossary

2CB hallucinogenic drug, also known as Nexus, that can cause frightening hallucinations in high doses. It is related to the drug ecstasy.

2C-T-7 strong synthetic hallucinogenic drug that can produce overwhelming visual hallucinations. In high doses it can cause death.

5-MeO-DiPT synthetic hallucinogenic drug with very variable effects

acid street name for the drug LSD

addiction when a person is dependent on (unable to manage without) a drug, and finds it extremely hard to stop

amphetamine type of stimulant drug, which speeds up the activity of the brain

AMT (alpha-methyltryptamine) type of synthetic hallucinogenic drug, which has effects that last from eight to fourteen hours

anaesthetic drug that removes the sensation of pain

bad trip unpleasant and sometimes frightening experience felt after taking LSD and other hallucinogens, including feelings of panic, confusion, and anxiety

blotter small square of paper with the drug LSD soaked into it

coma state of deep unconsciousness from which it is very hard to wake up

counsellor person trained to give advice and guidance to people to help resolve their problems

dealer person who buys and sells drugs illegally

dependence when a person is unable to cope without a drug

DMT (dimethyltriptamine) fast-acting hallucinogenic drug which produces a trip that usually lasts between ten minutes and an hour

DXM (dextromethorphan) drug found in some cough syrups and pills. Large doses can cause bad visual hallucinations and unconsciousness, and an overdose can result in coma and death.

flashback sudden and disturbing reoccurrence of some of the hallucinogenic effects of a trip. Flashbacks can bring back elements of a bad trip into a person's mind weeks, months, or even years after the initial trip.

fungus (pl. fungi) plant that does not have leaves, flowers, or roots, such as a mushroom

gelatine jelly-like substance

hallucination experience of seeing or hearing something that is not really present and only exists in the mind

hallucinogen substance that produces hallucinations

hippy term used mainly in the 1960s to describe someone of unconventional appearance – often with long hair and wearing jeans and beads. Many hippies experimented with hallucinogenic drugs.

in confidence privately, without telling anyone else

intoxicated under the influence of alcohol or another drug

ketamine synthetic anaesthetic drug that can cause hallucinations

magic mushroom fungus that has hallucinogenic properties and contains the chemicals psilocybin and psilocin. There are over 90 different kinds of magic mushroom. The most common is the Liberty Cap.

mescaline strong hallucinogenic drug extracted from the tops of the peyote cactus and also produced synthetically

Nexus hallucinogenic drug, also known as 2CB, that can cause frightening hallucinations in high doses. It is related to the drug ecstasy.

overdose excessive dose of a drug, which the body cannot cope with

panic attack sudden very strong feeling of anxiety, which makes a person's heart race

paranoia mental condition involving feelings of suspicion and distrust – a sense that everyone is out to get you, or to criticize your behaviour or actions

PCP (phencyclidine) synthetically produced hallucinogen, which has very unpleasant physical effects and can trigger violent behaviour, anxiety, and paranoia

pharmacist trained person who prepares and dispenses drugs

possession owning or having an illegal drug (either carrying it or having it hidden somewhere)

prescription medicine medical drug that can only be obtained when a patient has been given a written instruction form (a prescription), signed by a doctor or dentist

psychedelic relating to a drug such as LSD that causes hallucinations and increased sensitivity or perception

psychological to do with or affecting the mind, emotions, and behaviour

psychological dependence when a person feels they need drugs to get through everyday life and cannot cope without them

rave large party or gathering involving dancing, especially to electronic dance music

recreational use use of drugs on an occasional basis, especially when socializing

schizophrenia serious mental disorder that can lead to confused thinking and changes in a person's personality and behaviour

side effect unwanted effect of a drug or medical treatment

snort take a drug by sniffing it up the nose

supply give or sell drugs to other people

synthetic made artificially using chemicals

tab small square of paper with the drug LSD soaked into it

tolerance need for larger and larger doses of a drug to get the same effect

trip experience felt after taking a psychedelic drug, such as LSD or another hallucinogen, sometimes involving hallucinations

withdrawal symptoms unpleasant physical and mental feelings experienced during the process of giving up an addictive drug

Contacts and further information

There are a number of organizations that provide information and advice about drugs. Some have helpful websites, or provide information packs and leaflets, while others offer help and support over the phone.

Contacts in the UK

Adfam
Waterbridge House, 32–36 Loman Street, London SE1 0EH
Tel: 020 7928 8898
www.adfam.org.uk
Adfam is a national charity that gives confidential support and information to families and friends of drug users. They also run family support groups.

Connexions Direct
Helpline: 080 800 13219
(8 a.m.–2 a.m. daily)
Text: 07766 4 13219
www.connexions-direct.com
This service for teenagers offers information and advice on a wide range of topics, including drugs. Young people can also speak to an adviser by telephone, webchat, email, or text message.

DrugScope
32–36 Loman Street, London SE1 0EE
Tel: 020 7928 1211
www.drugscope.org.uk
A national drugs information agency with services that include a library, a wide range of publications, and a website.

Families Anonymous
Doddington & Rollo Community Association, Charlotte Despard Avenue, Battersea, London SW11 5HD
Helpline: 0845 1200 660
www.famanon.org.uk
An organization involved in support groups for parents and families of drug users. They can put you in touch with groups in different parts of the country.

FRANK
Tel: 0800 776600
Email: frank@talktofrank.com
www.talktofrank.com
An organization for young people that gives free, confidential advice and information about drugs 24 hours a day.

Narcotics Anonymous
UK Service Office, 202 City Road, London EC1V 2PH
Helpline: 020 7730 0009
(10 a.m.–10 p.m. daily)
www.ukna.org
A fellowship of people who have given up narcotics, using a twelve-step programme similar to the one used by Alcoholics Anonymous. They have a helpline for users and their friends and relatives, plus events and meetings around the United Kingdom.

Release
Helpline: 0845 4500 215
(10 a.m.–5.30 p.m. Mon–Fri)
Email: ask@release.org.uk
www.release.org.uk
An organization that provides legal advice to drug users, their families, and friends. The advice is free, professional, non-judgmental, and confidential.

Contacts in Australia and New Zealand

Alcohol & Other Drugs Council of Australia (ADCA)
17 Napier Close, Deakin, ACT 2600
Tel: 02 6281 1002
www.adca.org.au
ADCA works with the government and with community organizations to reduce the harm caused by drugs.

Australian Drug Foundation
409 King Street, West Melbourne, VIC 3003
Tel: 03 9278 8100
www.adf.org.au
An organization that works to prevent and reduce drug problems in the Australian community.

The DARE (Drug Abuse Resistance Education) Foundation of New Zealand
PO Box 50744, Porirua, New Zealand
Tel: 04 238 9550
www.dare.org.nz
An organization that provides drug prevention education programmes.

Foundation for Alcohol and Drug Education (FADE)
9 Anzac Street, PO Box 33–1505, Takapuna, Auckland, New Zealand
Tel: 09 489 1719
www.fade.org.nz
A national organization that provides services throughout the country.

Narcotics Anonymous
Australian Service Office, 1st Floor, 204 King Street, Newtown, NSW 2042
National helpline: 1300 652 820
http://na.org.au/
The Australian division of Narcotics Anonymous has helplines for users and their friends and relatives, plus events and meetings around Australia.

Turning Point
54–62 Gertrude Street, Fitzroy, VIC 3065
Helpline (DirectLine): 1800 888 236
www.turningpoint.org.au
Turning Point provides specialist treatment and support services to people affected by drug use.

Further reading

Dr Miriam Stoppard's Drug Information File: From Alcohol and Tobacco to Ecstasy and Heroin, by Miriam Stoppard (Dorling Kindersley, 1999)

Drugs and You, by Bridget Lawless (Heinemann Library, 2000)

Drugs: The Truth, by Aidan Macfarlane and Ann McPherson (Oxford University Press, 2003)

Health Issues: Drugs, by Sarah Lennard-Brown (Hodder Children's Books, 2004)

Need to Know: LSD, by Sean Connolly (Heinemann Library, 2000)

Teen Issues: Drugs, by Joanna Watson and Joanna Kedge (Raintree, 2004)

Why Do People Take Drugs?, by Patsy Westcott (Hodder Children's Books, 2000)

Wise Guides: Drugs, by Anita Naik (Hodder Children's Books, 1997)

Further research

If you want to find out more about problems related to hallucinogens, you can search the Internet, using a search engine such as Google. Try using keywords such as:

Hallucinogens + flashbacks
Hallucinogens + health
Hallucinogens + law
Hallucinogens + pregnancy

Disclaimer
All the Internet addresses (URLs) given in this book were valid at the time of going to press. However, owing to the dynamic nature of the Internet, some addresses may have changed or sites may have ceased to exist since publication. While the author, packager, and publishers regret any inconvenience this may cause readers, no responsibility for any such change can be accepted by the author, packager, or publishers.

Index

Titles in the *What's the Deal?* series include:

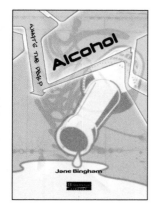

Hardback: 0431 107807

Hardback: 0431 107815

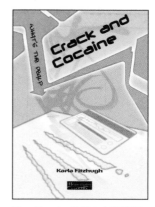

Hardback: 0431 107742

Hardback: 0431 107750

Hardback: 0431 107769

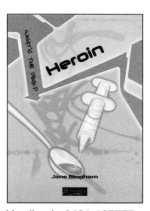

Hardback: 0431 107777

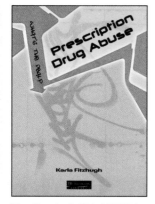

Hardback: 0431 107831

Hardback: 0431 10784X

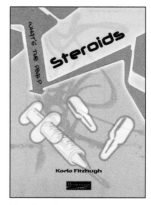

Hardback: 0431 107785

Find out about other titles from Heinemann Library on our website www.heinemann.co.uk/library